SHOJI HAMADA   MASTER POTTER

Edited by Timothy Wilcox

Foreword by Oliver Watson

With essays by Yuko Kikuchi, Julian Stair
and Timothy Wilcox and a Memoir by Janet Leach

SHOJI HAMADA MASTER POTTER

Lund Humphries Publishers, London
in association with Ditchling Museum, Sussex

First published in 1998 by
Lund Humphries Publishers
Park House
1 Russell Gardens
London NW11 9NN
in association with
Ditchling Museum, Sussex

on the occasion of the exhibitions at
Ditchling Museum, Sussex 4 April–7 June 1998
High Cross House, Dartington Hall, Devon
20 June–26 July 1998
Ashmolean Museum, Oxford 3–30 August 1998
Bonham's, London 4–17 September 1998

British Library Cataloguing in Publication Data
A catalogue record for this book is available from
the British Library

ISBN 0 85331 728 3

Distributed in the USA by
Antique Collectors' Club
Market Street Industrial Park
Wappingers Falls
NY 12590
USA

Designed by Ray Carpenter
Made and printed in Great Britain by
BAS Printers Limited, Over Wallop, Stockbridge,
Hampshire

Front cover:
Square vase 1960 (Cat.35)

Back cover:
Hamada's hands
(Photo: Tsune Sugimura)

Frontispiece:
Hamada glazing teabowls, 1970s
(Photo: Tsune Sugimura)

ABOUT THE CONTRIBUTORS

Yuko Kikuchi is Research Fellow at Chelsea
School of Art. She has published several articles
on the *Mingei* movement, and is joint author of
the exhibition catalogue *Ruskin in Japan*,
published in 1997.

Janet Leach was born in Texas in 1918. Already
trained as a potter, she witnessed Hamada's
demonstrations at Black Mountain College,
North Carolina, in 1952 and resolved to study in
Japan. She married Bernard Leach as his third
wife in 1956 and took over the running of the St
Ives Pottery, alongside her own career as a
maker of strong, highly individual pots.
Janet Leach died in 1997.

Julian Stair is one of Britain's leading potters
with work in many public collections including
the Victoria & Albert Museum, Sainsbury
Centre for the Visual Arts and the Boymans
Museum in Rotterdam. Since 1994, he has been
engaged in doctoral research into Critical
Writing in British Studio Pottery at the Royal
College of Art. At present he is Fellow in
Crafts and Criticism at the University of
Northumbria.

Dr Oliver Watson is Chief Curator of the
Department of Ceramics and Glass at the
Victoria & Albert Museum. He is the author of
the definitive catalogue, *British Studio Pottery:
the Victoria & Albert Museum Collection* and
in 1997 was curator of the exhibition *Bernard
Leach: Potter and Artist* shown at the Crafts
Council Gallery, London and on tour in Japan.

Timothy Wilcox is an art historian and
exhibition curator with interests including
British and French landscape painting as well as
the history of twentieth-century craft. He was
editor of the exhibition catalogue *Eric Gill and
the Guild of St Joseph and St Dominic* for Hove
Museum Art Gallery in 1989, and in 1997
curated the exhibition *Francis Towne
1739–1816* for the Tate Gallery, London.

CONTENTS

ACKNOWLEDGEMENTS

This exhibition came about through an exchange between Ditchling Museum and the Ceramic Art Centre in Mashiko, Japan. The work of the Ditchling craftsmen and women forms the centrepiece of an exhibition currently touring Japan, entitled *The English Arts & Crafts Movement and Hamada Shōji*. It was on the initiative of Hilary Bourne, Ditchling Museum's founder, that a reciprocal loan of objects from Japan was proposed.

A reassessment in Britain of Hamada's work is long overdue. Not since the exhibition at the Crafts Centre of Great Britain in 1963 has any survey of his work been presented here. The loan of a group of outstanding pieces from public and private collections in Mashiko has provided the impetus for the current exhibition, which, while far from comprehensive, will enable a new audience to experience something of the astonishing range of Hamada's creativity.

I am immensely grateful to Ditchling Museum for the invitation to curate this exhibition, and would like to extend my thanks to all those, far more familiar with this field than I, who have offered support, encouragement and practical assistance during its preparation. I am grateful to Margot Coatts, Edmund de Waal, Emmanuel Cooper, Alexander Bruce and Barley Roscoe for sharing their expertise; to Shinsaku Hamada, Tomoo Hamada, Ryūji Hamada and Wali Hawes for hospitality in Mashiko, Tokyo and Tokoname; to Kaene Yamada, Janet Rouse, Kyoko Utsumi Mimura and Adrian Hilton for assistance with the Japanese language. The curators of the British public collections, Moira Vincentelli, Hilary Williams, Tim Craven and Helen Simpson have generously responded to the numerous requests which accompany any agreement to lend. The Memoir by Janet Leach is printed by courtesy of the Trustees of the Leach Archive and the Holburne Museum and Crafts Study Centre, Bath (ref.10053).

At Lund Humphries, Lucy Myers and Anjali Raval have been the most sympathetic and accommodating of editors; I am most grateful to them, and to designer Ray Carpenter, for sharing in this project with such flair and enthusiasm. I would also like to thank David Leach, Kiko Noda, Smith and Mike O'Connor, Clare Clayton, Ewan Clayton and Kathy Niblett for their invaluable contributions.

Thanks to the enthusiasm of Hilary Williams, Oliver Impey and Cyril Frankel, the exhibition will be seen in three further venues; it is a pleasure to acknowledge the assistance of Sir Peter Wakefield and Katriana Hazell at Asia House for facilitating the latter two showings under their auspices. Assistance for the tour has been received from the Crafts Council; the catalogue and initiation costs in Ditchling have also been supported by the Japan Foundation, the Great Britain Sasakawa Foundation and South East Arts.

Timothy Wilcox
Ditchling

FOREWORD   HAMADA: POTTER

Oliver Watson

HAMADA's considerable lifelong achievements came from his work as a potter. The body of work he left incontrovertibly establishes him as one of the greatest artist-potters of the twentieth century. It was his pots that gave him a worldwide reputation, it was his desire to make pots that led him to set up in Mashiko, it was his devotion to quality in pots that made him a leader in the *Mingei* movement. This is in contrast to his friend Bernard Leach, where potting gave him the opportunity for expressing ideas and feelings that were often generated in other areas, and where writing and drawing played an important if not equal role.

Hamada has been an inspiration for generations of potters around the world as much in his practice and attitude to making as in the style of his pottery. But of course his practice and attitude were determined by his special qualities as a potter. And what exactly were his special qualities? It is an indication of Hamada's real talent as an artist that the qualities which were to distinguish him throughout his life are apparent in the earliest pots that he made. And these qualities again stand in remarkable contrast to those of his friend, and, at that time, mentor, Bernard Leach. Leach had trained as a graphic artist and had come to pottery relatively late in life. His graphic skills arguably equalled or even outweighed his ceramic skills. Not so with Hamada. His first works at St Ives show that relaxed and confident handling of clay which characterises all his work. Even more remarkably, his decoration in these early years was as forceful, as economic and as apt as it ever was in the mature artist. Unlike Leach, he was not frightened or disapproving of the spontaneous, the almost random or the accidental.

Hamada's importance for the history of studio ceramics in the UK cannot be overstated. We shall never know quite what moral support he gave Leach in those early years, though it was no doubt considerable. But it is clear that he played a major role in the establishment of the St Ives pottery, helping in both technical and artistic matters. He helped to design and fire the kiln and searched for suitable clays and fuel. His work helped raise the artistic profile of the pottery through exhibitions in London, given added interest in that they were the work of a 'genuine Oriental' potter. Later, in 1929, together with Yanagi, he encouraged Leach to join the Elmhirsts at Dartington, a move that certainly prevented the collapse of the Leach Pottery in St Ives. In 1952 his presence at the Dartington conference and his subsequent tour through the United States to Japan with Bernard Leach helped set the seal on the success of the *Mingei* approach to ceramics and helped confirm Leach as the leader of the studio pottery revival in Britain and further afield across the globe.

7

Unfortunately, collections of Hamada's pots in the UK are dispersed, small and tend to date from the pre-war period; these pieces can seem somewhat muted or restrained. There is nothing in this country that prepares the visitor for the experience one has in Japan when visiting, for example, the Mingeikan (the Japan Folk Crafts Museum in Tokyo) or the Ohara Museum in Kurashiki, where the spectacle of rows of large dishes with poured glaze decoration can be overwhelming. Nor in this country does one see many of the more colourful later works with overglaze enamel painting. Of necessity, much of our understanding of Hamada comes from reproductions in books and catalogues, yet he still retains his position. How much more impressive are the pots themselves, and how important it is that they are seen, for as Leach has said, '. . . the pot is the man; his virtues and vices are shown therein – no disguise is possible'.

Leach and Hamada at Mitsukoshi,
Tokyo in 1961
(Photo: Leach Archive, Holburne
Museum, Bath)

Timothy Wilcox

HEARTLAND:
SHOJI HAMADA AND DITCHLING

DURING HIS FIRST VISIT to England, from 1920 to 1923, Hamada spent almost all his time in St Ives. He had been invited by Bernard Leach to assist him in setting up the pottery there because of his solid scientific and technical training. Everything had to be learnt from the beginning; how to get the best from the available clay, what materials and recipes made suitable glazes, what sources of fuel were available for the kiln. The kiln itself, the first Japanese-style climbing kiln built in the West, caused problems of its own, and in 1922, an expert kiln builder, Matsubayashi, was summoned from Japan to rebuild it. As much as one-fifth of the production of the early firings was unusable and Hamada destroyed even more pieces if he was not satisfied with them. Despite this, he and Leach were relentlessly ambitious, seeking to recreate from the outset what they saw as the very highest achievements of the potter's art: the Chinese stonewares of the Sung Dynasty, with their range of subtle coloured glazes, and at the other end of the scale, the raw energy of early English slipware. The works included in Hamada's two London exhibitions in 1923 show that his interests extended beyond this, to inlaid porcelain (which he recreated in stoneware), Korean bottle shapes and the florid incised and relief decorated vases and bowls of Chinese Ts'u chou ware.

The intensity of the multiple demands of St Ives, not least the need to return an income on the money invested in the pottery, left the young Hamada little time for sightseeing. However, in St Ives, at the home of Mrs Podmore, one of the customers of the pottery, he saw an example of weaving by Ethel Mairet. Mairet had settled in Ditchling in Sussex in 1918; besides her work as a handweaver, she was the leading pioneer in the revival of natural dyeing. In 1916, her manual *A Book on Vegetable Dyes* had been published by Hilary Pepler in Hammersmith. Pepler preceded Mairet in moving to Ditchling, arriving there with his family later in 1916 and embarking on a new career as a handprinter. He joined the calligrapher Edward Johnston and the letter-cutter and sculptor Eric Gill as the third member of a little band of creative and highly individual talents dedicated to seeking an alternative route out of the impasse of industrialism and its consequences, of which the war then being conducted in Europe was only the most appalling example.

Among the earliest publications of St Dominic's Press, as Pepler's Ditchling press soon became known, was a pamphlet by Mairet and her husband, Philip, entitled *An Essay on Crafts and Obedience*. After a lament on the lack of spiritual values in present-day craftsmanship (most likely contributed by Philip) there followed Mairet's more practical reflections on the need for thorough workshop training and on the value of tradition: 'But tradition is a living force and we must be fully conscious that we are building tradition.'[1] Mairet had experienced such living tradition at first hand when she accompanied her first husband, Ananda K. Coomaraswamy, to Ceylon in 1903–6, where he was researching and writing *Medieval Sinhalese Art*, his authoritative account of the island's arts and crafts. On their return to England, the couple lived in Broad Campden within the orbit of C. R. Ashbee's Guild of Handicraft, where the co-operative spirit of the Arts & Crafts ideal had for a time been most nearly realised. In later life, Mairet was to become an avid collector of ethnic textiles, especially in Eastern Europe, where the same continuity of tradition could still be found.

Leach and Hamada came to Ditchling in November 1921 to visit Ethel Mairet and see

Ditchling in 1920
From a postcard of the period
Ditchling Museum

something of what was at that time the most dynamic and diverse manifestation of the Arts & Crafts Movement still to be found in England. Leach's pocket appointments diary for 1921, following the note, 'Mr Mairet/Zen articles', entered at 23 November, includes a list of names, presumably of all those he encountered: 'Mr & Mrs Mairet/Douglas Pepler/Eric Gill/Edward Johnston/David Jones/Desmond Chute/Mr & Mrs Chettle/Mr Fred Partridge/ Miss Maud Partridge'.[2] Chettle was a local architect and builder, and supporter of the crafts; the last two were Ethel Mairet's brother and sister, Fred a well-established woodworker and jeweller, Maud a weaver in Mairet's workshop. Leach was also able to look up his old etching master, the reclusive Frank Brangwyn, who since 1918 was another resident in Ditchling.

The exact length of the potters' stay in Ditchling is not known, but it was unlikely to have been more than a few days. On 6 November, a Sunday, Eric Gill noted in his diary, 'Mairet brought some friends to see me in eve – Bernard Leach & a Japanese friend Hamada Sanji [sic] they stayed to supper'.[3] The following morning the visitors returned to see the workshops which had recently been built for the Guild of St Joseph and St Dominic on land behind Gill's house on Ditchling Common. Pepler's press occupied one central block; there was a sculpture shop for Gill and his assistant Joseph Cribb, and another for Desmond Chute, Gill's young pupil and confidant who would shortly leave to pursue a vocation to the Catholic priesthood. Opposite the workshops was the small chapel in which the guild members, all practising Catholics, met to say or sing the daily offices.[4]

It was not the overt expression of religious commitment so much as the practical aspects of the life of the Guild which appear to have most impressed Hamada. The guild aimed at more than the reform of working conditions: it saw itself as creating a counter-culture in miniature, following the Distributist ideals propounded by the Catholic apologist, Hilaire Belloc, and the Dominican prior, Father Vincent McNabb. Animals kept on the land provided food; there were bees for honey, and home-brewed beer. Hamada later recalled: 'Seeing the lifestyle of Mrs Ethel Mairet and Eric Gill confirmed my conviction about living in the country upon returning to Japan.'[5]

Hamada's identification with the Ditchling crafts community found a concrete expression the following year, 1922, when he ordered a suit made of Mairet's cloth. Then, in November 1923, just before his second exhibition opened in London, Hamada returned to Ditchling.[6] Apparently, he hoped to acquire another suit of Mairet's tweed, but the cloth was not available. Instead, he was given a suit already made up for Mairet's husband, Philip; the weaver could have been Valentine KilBride. Mairet was largely self-taught as a weaver and her skills were limited; much that was sold under her name was produced by her apprentices or by hired workers. In 1923, one of these was KilBride, a Bradford-trained weaver who had recently arrived in Ditchling enquiring about membership of the Guild. Following his acceptance in 1925, he remained one of its pillars until his death in 1982. On his marriage in December 1924, Hamada wore one of these suits, a gesture which is even more significant in the light of his lifelong adherence to traditional Japanese dress in Mashiko.

Examples of Mairet's weaving were sent back to Japan along with pieces of English slipware; together, they commemorated all that most attracted him in the place. The selection recognised the combination of ancient and modern as a unity, rather than as opposites, which became characteristic of Hamada's own mature aesthetic and the whole philosophy of *Mingei*. Mairet's use of traditional English pottery made a great impression on Hamada. 'When Leach and I visited Mrs Mairet, the mother of English hand-weaving, in Ditchling, Sussex, she served us dinner using a complete set of slipware which I have never forgotten. The dishes were products of Fishley, a potter who preserved the good traditions of England, the last one to do so. His slipware was often put on display in the market and sold there. The large and small pitchers, oval dishes, and green plates all went well with the large oak table. When you are invited to dinner by someone, you often notice, as a potter, that dishes of lower quality are used together with superior pieces. But Mrs Mairet served food on the best dishes, a perfect score.'[7]

In August 1929, on his next visit to England, Hamada returned once again to Ditchling, bringing with him Sōetsu Yanagi. They went to Mairet's workshop at Gospels, where Yanagi, in particular, took a great interest in the handspinning and use of natural dyes; both men bought quantities of cloth. They also went to the guild workshops on Ditchling Common. Gill had now departed, but KilBride was there, now fully established as a weaver in partnership with Bernard Brocklehurst. Hamada ordered 60 yards of their woollen tweed, half 'coating' and half 'suiting', for which he paid £44.2.0, a considerable sum. Two weeks later, on paying for the first order, he ordered a further 17 yards of 'handspun suiting' for £10.7.0. This was despatched to Japan after his departure via the Trans-Siberian Railway.

HAND-WEAVER

Mrs Mairet, Gospels,
DITCHLING
Hand-spun, Hand-woven & vegetable dyed woollens, silks and Cottons, Jerkins, Skirt lengths, Scarfs, Children's Dresses
Dyeing and Spinning
LESSONS GIVEN

Advertisement for Ethel Mairet's weaving
From a Ditchling Guide of 1926
Ditchling Museum

Ethel Mairet weaving
Woodcut. Artist unknown. From a Ditchling Guide of 1926
Ditchling Museum

Another acquaintanceship revived on this occasion must have been that of Edward Johnston. 'Both Hamada and Yanagi said that he was the most remarkable man they had met in England. No one taught by him forgot his timeless purity,' Leach later recalled.[8] Hamada requested an example of Johnston's calligraphy to be sent to Japan at the time of the opening of the Folk Crafts Museum in 1936.

Leach also recognised the value of the Ditchling enterprise; however, when it came to the building of a new model society, his involvement was to be at Dartington. It was Pepler's St Dominic's Press which printed Leach's *A Potter's Outlook* as one of a series of Handworkers' Pamphlets in 1928; in this little tract some of the ideas more fully worked out in *A Potter's Book* were first expressed in print. On his return from Japan in 1935, Leach spent months living in a caravan while that book was drafted, some of this time in a field on the downs overlooking Ditchling.

After 1929, Hamada did not visit Britain again until 1952, on the occasion of the International Conference on Pottery and Textiles at Dartington. Following intensive sessions listening to papers, the final evening was spent in folk dancing, but this was not an aspect of traditional culture in which Hamada was prepared to indulge. One living art which he did maintain, though, was cookery. A recipe for Cornish pasties brought back from St Ives in 1923 is still in use in his family today, the authentic taste perfectly preserved. In Ditchling, Hamada found a crafts community in which the surroundings, the buildings and the human activity seemed to be at one; this unity, this same wholeness, is what he determined to create in Mashiko.

1. Quoted in M. Coatts, *A Weaver's Life: Ethel Mairet, 1872–1952*, p.55.
2. Leach Papers, Holburne Museum, Bath.
3. Eric Gill Diary, Clark Library, University of California, Los Angeles. Microfilm in the Tate Gallery Archive, London.
4. See the exhibition catalogue *Eric Gill and the Guild of St Joseph and St Dominic*, Hove Museum & Art Gallery, 1989.
5. B. Leach, *Hamada, Potter*, p.80.
6. The visit is recorded in Eric Gill's Diary, 11 November 1923.
7. Ibid, p.59.
8. B. Leach, *Beyond East and West*, pp.211–12.

Julian Stair

GENIUS AND CIRCUMSTANCE:
EARLY CRITICISM OF HAMADA'S POTTERY
IN ENGLAND

SHOJI HAMADA AND BERNARD LEACH arrived in 1920 to an England critically receptive to Orientalism. Enthusiasm for Chinese antiquities was at an unprecedented level and, in the art world, this was directly connected to an emergent British Modernism and its interest in the 'primitive'.

A decade earlier, an editorial on Oriental art in *The Burlington Magazine*, probably written by Roger Fry, the arch Modernist of the period, stated that:

> There are signs that the present rapidly increasing preoccupation with Oriental art will be more intense, and produce a profounder impression on our views, than any previous phase of Orientalism. For one thing, we are more disillusioned, more tired with our tradition, which seems to have landed us at length in a too frequent representation of the obvious or the sensational. To us the art of the East presents the hope of discovering a more spiritual, more expressive idea of design.[1]

The myths surrounding Hamada's and Leach's early years in England are numerous. The imposing Leach, accompanied by his quiet friend, have been seen as evangelical figures attempting to convert the English to the values of Oriental pottery, in particular that of the Sung Dynasty. In fact the converse was true. By 1920 Sung Dynasty pottery was already well known, almost in vogue. A series of seven articles had been published in *The Burlington Magazine* on 'Wares of the Sung and Yuan Dynasties' by R. L. Hobson, the renowned British Museum curator. The Burlington Fine Arts Club Summer Exhibition of 1910 was devoted to Chinese pottery of the Sung and Ming Dynasties. The Clarendon Press published a translation of the highly eclectic *T'ao Shuo*[2] in the same year which was a compilation of writing from 'the old prose authors and poets of the T'ang and other dynasties',[3] while Korean ceramics were also discussed in many articles in, for example, *The Burlington Magazine* in 1912.[4] New archaeological excavations in China in the immediate pre- and post-war periods were eagerly received in the West and helped establish the provenance of this early pottery, 'wonderful' finds that 'the present century has for the first time brought to the knowledge of the Western world'.[5] Scholarly interest developed to such an extent in the period before Hamada's and Leach's arrival that in 1917 Bernard Rackham, Keeper of the Ceramics Department at the Victoria & Albert Museum, even wrote a survey of critical literature on Chinese pottery.[6]

Interest in Orientalism was not limited to scholars and academics. It was also significant to the British avant garde, in its mediation of French Post-Impressionism's fascination with the 'primitive', which extended from Van Gogh's homage to Japanese prints through to Picasso's and Matisse's interest in African art. The connection between ancient Oriental and modern art was furthered by collectors such as Mr Kelekian, 'the greatest collector and dealer in Oriental textiles and pottery', who moved on to collect modern art. Roger Fry wrote in 1920: 'Mr Kelekian's venture in modern art is of comparatively recent date . . . His long familiarity with early Oriental art has trained his taste . . . in his choice of modern work.'[7] The famous 17th-century Japanese potter Koetsu's work was illustrated in the second, final issue of Wyndham Lewis's journal *Blast* in 1915. The antithesis of the anonymous Oriental craftsman later promoted by Leach, Hamada and Yanagi, Koetsu's work influenced the alternative approach to Oriental ceramics taken by another great potter of the inter-war years, William Staite Murray.

Chinese pottery featured in specialist exhibitions such as 'Early Ting Ware' at the Victoria & Albert Museum in 1922, but Oriental art had also become a viable financial proposition for many commercial galleries in London such as Messrs Bluett and Sons, John Sparks, Yamaka's, Ton Ying and Co and Knoedler's Galleries. In 1930 *The Burlington Magazine* revealed the extent of this popularity: 'Evidently there is no decline of interest in the material products of Chinese civilisation. The two exhibitions last month were crowded and seldom before have displays been so diversified and of such high excellence.'[8] Paterson's Gallery also showed early Chinese art. In reviewing an exhibition there in 1920 R. L. Hobson wrote: 'Carefully selected and tastefully arranged it comprises many of the most attractive types of Han, Tang, Sung and Ming wares . . . The Sung representatives include many rare and choice examples.'[9] It was understandable that Paterson's should exhibit Hamada only three years later in 1923, for in many ways he was the living embodiment of 'Orientalism'. The very first solo show of contemporary studio pottery in a Bond Street gallery, this established a precedent for subsequent exhibitions of all the major English studio potters of the decade – Bernard Leach, William Staite Murray, Reginald Wells, Charles Vyse, Katherine Pleydell Bouverie and Nora Braden.

Shōji Hamada received generous critical coverage in the British press by the standards of the 1920s. In total, his four exhibitions at Paterson's generated three reviews in *The Times*, two in *The Spectator*, catalogue essays from Leach and Yanagi and numerous references in general articles on studio pottery. The first reference to Hamada was in December 1920, shortly after his arrival in Britain. It was a less than auspicious start. He was described in *The Pottery Gazette and Glass Trade Review* as Bernard Leach's 'Japanese assistant, Mr Hamada' who had 'studied from the scientific side at the Kyoto Governmental Experimental Pottery Works'.[10] The article was 'specially contributed', probably by Leach himself and it effectively placed Hamada at the level of a technician. Three years later this had changed. Hamada's one-man show at Paterson's Gallery was reviewed in *The Spectator*, in which he was referred to as 'a Japanese potter of considerable reputation in Japan, at present working at Mr Leach's pottery in St Ives . . .'[11] These early references encapsulate Hamada's short time in England – the positive acceptance of his work and the rapid progression of his relationship with Leach from 'assistant' to 'collaborator' to 'friend'.

Chinese pottery was the benchmark for virtually all studio pottery in the 1920s: 'It is said that a man cannot paint who has not studied the Italians; no more can a potter pot who is unversed in Sung.'[12] Given the early stage in the development of studio pottery at a time when it was completely reliant on Oriental models, comparisons were inevitable. In the first reviews by the critic W. McCance in *The Spectator*, Hamada was seen as a potter who 'concentrates on recapturing old traditional effects in glaze',[13] while Charles Marriot in *The Times* commented: 'In general the shapes are in the Chinese tradition.' These comparisons persisted until Hamada's last show in 1931 in which his maturing work caused Marriot to reflect: 'Oddly enough, his work in general seems to owe less to the Chinese than that of some of our English potters – a case of natural, as compared with adoptive descent, one supposes.'[14]

Hamada was seen as a potter of integrity by his reviewers. Even in comparison with Kawai and Tomimoto, Japanese contemporaries of his who also showed in London,

Hamada's work had 'sturdy strength . . . a deeper artistic impulse'.[15] This theme of solidity recurred throughout many of the British reviews of Hamada's work. Epithets such as 'economy' and 'simple' were commonly used although Marriot thought the pots 'blunt' and 'just a little lacking in subtlety'.[16] In W. McCance's fascinating review of 1923, following Hamada's second show of stoneware at Paterson's Gallery, he made a revealing comparison of Hamada's and Leach's work. In one of the first attempts to place pottery in a modern critical context, McCance described Leach as 'a potter with a bias towards painting . . . he coaxes the mass of inert clay . . . works delicately with his fingers',[17] while Hamada, with a bias towards sculpture, 'compels it, by pressure, into aesthetic equilibrium, . . . uses his hands more as a whole'. McCance concluded that 'Mr Leach's [pots] have more of grace, Mr Hamada's more of power.' In comparing the two potters' use of surface decoration, McCance perceptively remarked: 'In this superaddition of pattern to form, pottery differs from either painting or sculpture.' Tellingly, he omitted Leach completely. He noted: 'Mr Hamada has adapted the same basic pattern to a variety of shapes; it becomes a new pattern and an integral part.' McCance was probably hinting at Leach's tendency to rely on pictorial motifs while Hamada could make 'pattern synthesize with form'.

Charles Marriot also discussed Hamada's skill as a decorator and his use of calligraphy. Making tactful comparisons with other English potters, he wrote: 'What most obviously distinguishes it from the work of our potters who have studied Oriental methods is the superiority of the brush decoration, broad and free but controlled in a way that is only possible to a trained calligrapher.'[18] Marriot unfortunately also revealed the limits of his appreciation of Hamada's flair for decoration: 'Occasionally, . . . he seems to make mistakes – applying a rectangular pattern to a circular surface.'

Hamada's association with Leach and their shared interest in English pottery also created an opportunity for writers on studio pottery to discuss Occidental influences. It was noted in Hamada's pots that 'in form and decoration Western models have occasionally been adopted'[19] and 'English influences – particularly in slip decoration are apparent . . . but thoroughly digested.'[20] At times, however, critical comment seemed to be motivated more by a sense of wounded pride than an interest in the underlying issues: 'Mr Hamada . . . was attracted to the craft of potting through having seen examples of an English potter's work.'[21] Charles Marriot was always keen to reveal English influences and wrote how 'Mr Hamada's experiences at St Ives broadened and enriched his art'.[22] Despite the Occidental influence Marriot saw in Hamada's work, he failed to comment on the fact that his 'Tea-set for six', made in Japan for an English audience, was completely alien to Japanese pottery.

One of the most significant themes of the decade was the importance of materials in the making of pottery. Comments on Hamada's methods varied from Marriot's travelogue of local materials – 'china clay from Towednack and red clay from St Erth' – to the more enquiring approach of McCance in his understanding of historical precedents for 'truth to materials'. 'The older Chinese and Japanese potters understood the value of what are at present called impurities . . . [which] must be understood in order to be used to advantage.'[23] Although Leach did not write about materials in his catalogue essay of 1929, he noted that Hamada's first exhibition marked a stage where 'there no longer existed a technical barrier between ancient and modern'.[24] Yanagi's crusade for the use of unrefined materials was emphasised in his catalogue essay of 1931 in which he stated: 'Few understand that the beauty of ceramics is mainly the beauty of materials,'[25] and he contrasted this with the 'delusion that nature can be refined'.

Although the timing of Hamada's arrival in England was fortuitous, the extent and quality of press coverage of his work was undoubtedly deserved. During the three years he worked at St Ives he embodied the phenomenal interest in Orientalism and authenticated the artistic ideals of the period. Prophetically, Bernard Leach recorded a conversation with Yanagi six years before returning to England in which 'Y. asked me if I thought an artistic period in history is due to genius or circumstance. I replied that both were necessary.'[26] In the formulation of craft in the 1920s, Hamada supplied the genius and the emerging British studio pottery movement the circumstance.

Shōji Hamada
Bull charger c.1921–3
Earthenware with slip decoration.
Diam: 41 cm
The Bergen Collection, Stoke-on-Trent
City Museum & Art Gallery

1. 'Oriental Art', *The Burlington Magazine*, Vol.XVII, No.LXXXV, April 1910.
2. *Description of Chinese Pottery and Porcelain*, being a translation of the *T'ao Shuo* with an introduction, notes and bibliography, Stephen Bushall. Oxford: Clarendon Press, 1910.
3. Ibid.
4. Raphael Petrucci, 'Corean Pottery', *The Burlington Magazine*, Vol.XXII, No.CXVI, Nov. 1912.
5. 'The Pottery Figures of Mr Charles Vyse', *The Studio*, Vol.81, May 1921.
6. Bernard Rackham, 'The Literature of Chinese Pottery : A Brief Survey and Review', *The Burlington Magazine*, Vol.XXX, No.CLXVII, Feb. 1917.
7. Roger Fry, 'Modern Paintings in a Collection of Ancient Art', *The Burlington Magazine*, Vol.XXXVII, No.CCXIII, Dec. 1920.
8. 'Two Exhibitions of Chinese Art', *The Burlington Magazine*, Vol.LVII, No.CLCXXVIII, July 1930.
9. R. L. Hobson, 'Early Chinese Art at Paterson's Gallery', *The Burlington Magazine*, Vol.XXXVII, No.CCXIV, Aug. 1920.
10. 'An Art Pottery in Cornwall' (Specially Contributed), *The Pottery Gazette and Glass Trade Review*, p.1661, 1 December 1920.
11. W. McCance, 'The Pottery of Mr. Shōji Hamada', *The Spectator*, 26 May 1923.
12. W. A. Thorpe, 'English Stoneware Pottery by Miss K. Pleydell Bouverie and Miss D. K. N. Braden', *Artwork*, Vol.6, No.24, Winter 1930.
13. McCance, op. cit.
14. Charles Marriot, 'Two Potters', *The Times*, 10 November 1931.
15. Anon, 'Some Modern Pottery', *Artwork*, Vol.5, No.19, Autumn 1929.
16. Marriot, op. cit.
17. McCance, op. cit.
18. Charles Marriot, 'A Japanese Potter', *The Times*, 24 May 1929.
19. Anon, op. cit.
20. Charles Marriot, 'Two Potters', *The Times*, 10 November 1931.
21. 'Mr Shōji Hamada's Exhibition of Stoneware Pottery at Mr W. M. Paterson's Gallery', *Apollo*, Vol.IX, No.54, June 1929.
22. Charles Marriot, 'A Japanese Potter', *The Times*, 24 May 1929.
23. McCance, op. cit.
24. *Shōji Hamada, Bernard Leach*, exhibition catalogue, Paterson's Gallery, May to June 1929.
25. M. Yanagi, 'The Pottery of Shōji Hamada', exhibition catalogue, Paterson's Gallery, Oct. to Nov. 1931.
26. Bernard Leach, 'A Review, 1909–1914', Tokyo, 1914.

Yuko Kikuchi

HAMADA AND
THE *MINGEI* MOVEMENT

Shoji Hamada was one of the pioneer artist-potters in modern Japan and one of the most important core members of the *Mingei* (Japanese Folkcrafts) movement. In co-operation with Kenkichi Tomimoto, Bernard Leach, Kanjirō Kawai and Sōetsu Yanagi, Hamada created a 'hybrid' *Mingei* theory which appropriated modern aesthetic ideas such as 'art of the people', 'primitive', 'medieval', 'Oriental art' and 'national art' from Europe, particularly England, into the Japanese context, eventually formulating the 'criterion of beauty' through Japanese folkcrafts.[1] Reflecting Japanese society in search of Japanese-style 'modernisation', the *Mingei* movement successfully demonstrated 'modernity' interwoven with the discourse of national cultural identity.

Hamada's 'modernity' began with his early ambition to be a Western-style painter. He was among many young artists who recognised 'modernity' in the ideas of 'individual originality' and 'freedom of expression' common to the Post-Impressionists and Fauvists. These ideas were eagerly translated and interpreted in the influential *Shirakaba*.[2] Hamada was also an enthusiastic watercolourist.[3] This so-called Japanese 'watercolour' movement was initially triggered by British artists who visited Japan. Watercolour was an accessible and popular amateur medium in which to discover the native Japanese landscape through open-air painting, with a modern discourse about 'national art' similar to *Nihonga* (Japanese-style painting).[4]

A crucial turning-point which diverted Hamada's interest from painting to pottery was his encounter with works by Bernard Leach and Kenkichi Tomimoto in the Mikasa Gallery, Ginza, in 1912. As they had done in the Bijutsu Shinpō exhibition at Gorakuden in Tokyo, in 1911, Leach and Tomimoto at that time were experimenting with pottery as part of their broad interest in work that included interior design – a project inspired by Morris and English Arts & Crafts aesthetics. Such experiments demonstrated modern concepts of 'art of the people' in a Japanese context. Captivated by the 'modernity' of these works, with their 'hybrid' Oriental and Occidental style evident in form and design,[5] Hamada called them 'grand champions' who 'opened many windows' with new ideas and served as 'perfect measures'[6] by which to evaluate himself as an artist-potter.

The 'modernity' Hamada sought in the notion of a hybrid of Occident and Orient was also vividly described in his detailed observations concerning lifestyle. He was extremely impressed by Tomimoto's whole 'hybrid' lifestyle with 'an air of sophistication' in the remote Japanese countryside.[7] When Hamada visited Leach in Abiko in 1919, he was even more impressed by Yanagi's 'hybrid' lifestyle,[8] with Leach's Chinese-style studio, and notably a quilted rug in the studio inspired by *jūdō* wear and by the garden furniture in Japanese cedar, all designed by Leach himself. He found in Leach's lifestyle 'the truest way to live out this particular period, this time of history'.[9] Moreover, it was the time when the social and domestic reform movement was gaining ground under the slogan *bunka seikatsu* (culture life), signifying a rational, modern, Occidental lifestyle for the urban masses. Through interior and furniture design, co-operative housing projects and garden city planning, designers were adopting a Japanese version of Western 'modernity' to create an original 'hybrid' style.

By the late 1920s, at the moment of the full flowering of the social and domestic reform movement, the *Mingei* theory, with its core ideas of 'criterion of beauty', was created by Yanagi and demonstrated to the public an example of total lifestyle through their modern, ad-hoc, ethical hybrid style. In 1928, a medievalistic craft guild called *Kamigamo Mingei Kyōdan* (Kamigamo Crafts Communion) was established, with Yanagi's encouragement, by four craftsmen. They and other artist-craftsmen associated with the *Mingei* movement designed the interior and exterior of the Folkcrafts Pavilion, later called *Mikunisō*, and exhibited at the Imperial Exposition. Hamada contributed pots, the design of a fireplace and surrounding tiles and lampshades, emphasising his experience in England of the English ethical ideal of modern rural living, absorbed through the lifestyles of Eric Gill and Ethel Mairet.[10]

As Leach and Tomimoto had done earlier, Hamada at this time also displayed interest in the design of furniture and interiors, and, indeed, in the entire living environment. A dining table and benches in zelkova wood, designed by him in 1923, exemplify a hybrid of English medieval form with Japanese wood and finish. Chairs were also of particular interest to those involved in the *Mingei* movement. Tomimoto wrote *Isu no Hanashi* ('The Story of Chairs') and himself designed many chairs, while Yanagi was an avid collector of Windsor chairs. Hamada was impressed by Leach's three-legged chair of Japanese cedar in his own peculiar 'hybrid' style,[11] and another chair upholstered with material inspired by the Japanese fireman's quilted coat, which he described as 'very close to life, to living, and

A dining table and benches designed
by Hamada, c.1923
Zelkova wood.
Table 222 cm long, benches 177 and
181 cm long.
Mashiko Reference Collection

A fireplace designed by Hamada

very exotic and unusual'.[12] During his stay in England, Hamada collected Windsor and rush-bottomed chairs, and experimented in designing chairs with Leach.[13] In Japan, chairs were by now important objects for *bunka seikatsu*, symbolising Western culture, 'rational' living and modernity, and many designers created them as an expression of the 'hybrid' style, as an integral part of Japanese modern living.

Hamada found another important form of 'modernity' in the crafts of Okinawa, acknowledging, 'my work began in England, learned much in Okinawa, and matured in Mashiko'.[14] Okinawa, a group of islands lying to the south of Japan, was annexed to Japan in 1879. Modern Okinawan studies were then initiated by European and Japanese anthropologists, and in the twentieth century were absorbed into the broader spectrum of Japanese cultural studies. Among the people who were involved in the *Mingei* movement, Hamada and Kawai were the first to 'discover' Okinawan culture on their visit in 1918. Hamada also spent several winters in Okinawa after his marriage in 1924. For an élite college graduate urban potter like Hamada, the culture of Okinawa was a real revelation. He was impressed by the 'healthy', 'correct' work exemplified by the *namban jar*[15] produced from the 'real true life' in Tsuboya pottery,[16] which he felt trivialised the superiorities of his technical knowledge.

Hamada's 'discovery' of Okinawa must have nourished Yanagi during the process of formulating *Mingei* theory. Twenty years later, Yanagi himself visited Okinawa and wrote numerous articles on its crafts and culture during the late 1930s to 1940s which made a significant contribution to the later development of the *Mingei* movement. Yanagi eloquently articulated the 'supreme beauty' of Okinawan crafts by applying to them his 'criterion of beauty', and further enlarged upon his political discourse of 'innate and original Japaneseness' in the view he adopted of Okinawan crafts as a Japanese cultural archive.[17]

Hamada greatly contributed to the *Mingei* movement throughout the period from its formation to its completion. Unlike Tomimoto and Kawai,[18] he remained its most devoted member and was a loyal colleague to Yanagi. After the Second World War, when Yanagi developed his *Mingei* theory into his so-called 'Buddhist aesthetics', Hamada played an important role as a practical maker, demonstrating the creative process controlled naturally by the 'unconscious', 'no-mindedness' and 'other power' (*tariki*) which Yanagi stressed in his writing.[19] Together with Yanagi and Leach, Hamada's work made a strong visual impact on people both at home and abroad. The co-operative activities of the *Mingei* movement found expression as an 'esoteric', 'authentic' and 'traditional' form of Oriental aesthetics. Hamada became the model potter, his objects the epitome of *Mingei*, fulfilling its criteria in being described variously as 'simple', 'healthy', 'round', 'robust', 'secure' and 'peaceful'. Yanagi also praised Hamada's works as 'honest and healthy' functional ware created in a natural country environment; furthermore, he admired his unsigned works as a sign of 'relying on *tariki*'.[20]

However, at the same time, Hamada was expressing his own opinion which revealed a different attitude. His comment on Kawai's works is ambivalent and different from Yanagi who criticised Kawai's works as 'gaudy' and 'over-decorated',[21] straying from the true path of *Mingei*.[22] He pointed to Kawai's 'mistreatment' and 'weakness' as a result of not fully relying on *tariki*, but nevertheless defended him and Tomimoto, declaring that 'people such as Kawai and Tomimoto have trodden their true path, they have eaten folkcrafts and then have developed their own path. This is legitimate, the natural thing, for them.'[23]

Hamada revealed the inner struggle between his role as a model potter in the *Mingei* movement and his other self as a progressive artist. He may well have wished to carry out more radical experiments but it became increasingly difficult when his style became established as synonymous with the *Mingei* style. In exchange for fame and security, he may have given up his chance to explore his 'originality' with broader experiments as Kawai or Tomimoto did. He compensated with a rigorous attitude to his pupil Shimaoka, who recalled Hamada's repeated criticisms of his work, pointing out the lack of 'originality' and 'adventure'.[24] Hamada's search for 'modernity' was confused and diverted by the establishment of the *Mingei* movement.

1. Y. Kikuchi, 'Hybridity and the Oriental Orientalism of *Mingei* Theory', *Journal of Design History*, Vol.10, No.4, 1997, pp.343–54.
2. *Shirakaba* was published from 1910 to 1923 by the school of writers who included Saneatsu Mushanokoji, Naoya Shiga, three Arishima brothers: Takeo Arishima, Ikuma Arishima and Ton Satomi, Sōetsu Yanagi, Rigen Kinoshita, Kinyuki Sonoike, Kikuo Kojima, Yoshirō Nagayo and Torahiko Kōri, who were all from Gakushūin Kōtōka. They played a pioneering role in introducing 'modern' art and literature from the West.
3. S. Hamada, *Kama ni Makasete*, p.34.
4. See Y. Kikuchi and T. Watanabe, *Ruskin in Japan 1890–1940: Nature for Art, Art for Life*, Tokyo, 1997, pp.287–97.
5. S. Hamada, op. cit., p.42.
6. B. Leach, *Hamada*, Tokyo, New York, San Francisco, 1981 (1975), p.35.
7. Hamada, op. cit., p.71; Leach, op. cit., p.22.
8. Leach, op. cit., p.22.
9. Hamada, op. cit., pp.72–3; Leach, ibid., p.26.
10. Hamada, 'Gill Homon' (A Visit to Gill), *Kōgei*, No.31, 1933, pp.37–43.
11. Leach, op. cit., p.26.
12. Leach, ibid., p.24.
13. Leach, ibid., pp.119–22.
14. K. Yoshida, 'The Ceramic Art of Shōji Hamada' in *The Retrospective Exhibition of Shōji Hamada*, Tokyo, 1977, p.15.
15. There are two types of pot produced in Tsuboya pottery; one is called *arayachi* (unglazed rough ware) and the other is *jōyachi* (enamel glazed ware). *Namban* jars are in the former group.
16. S. Hamada, 'Tsuboya no Shigoto', *Kōgei*, No.99, 1939, pp.50–6.
17. Kikuchi, op. cit.
18. Tomimoto's relationship with Yanagi soured in the late 1920s and he left the movement. Kawai gradually distanced himself from the movement and his works were often criticised by Yanagi and Leach.
19. Leach, op. cit., pp.136–7.
20. Sōetsu Yanagi, *Collected Works of Sōetsu Yanagi*, Vol.14, Tokyo, 1981, pp.227–8.
21. Ibid., p.160.
22. Yanagi, op. cit., Vol.14, p.185.
23. Leach, op. cit., p.124.
24. T. Shimaoka, 'Waga Shi Hamada Sensei' (My Teacher Hamada) in *Mashiko no Chichi Ningen Kokuhō Hamada Shōji* (Father of Mashiko, Living National Treasure Shōji Hamada), Tokyo, 1976, pp.164–7.

Janet Leach

IMPRESSIONS OF MR HAMADA, HIS POTTERY AND LIFE AT MASHIKO, 1954

IT IS QUITE DIFFICULT to describe impressions of pottery at Mr Hamada's in Mashiko or to make broad generalisations which give the proper picture because what Mr Hamada teaches us, by example, is that of Spirit of Approach with the technical factors merely fitting themselves into the overall picture. After having been in Mashiko with Mr Hamada for a few months, I find myself constantly contrasting the life and work here with that of American potters and begin to realise the unrewarding amount of labour and element of struggle which enters into our Western lives and into our efforts to produce good pottery, from which we reap only a small return of pots, good and bad.

The day I arrived in Mashiko, 9 June, was a memorable one. The beauty of the place is far beyond anything I have experienced: traditional houses of adobe-like stucco with heavy wooden beams and thick thatched roofs, sitting on a hillside overlooking a valley of rice paddies (they were planting when I arrived) and a ridge of hills on the horizon with a spine of trees silhouetted against the sky. Tucked inconspicuously amid the formal garden and along the paths between the houses are many examples of Korean sculpture, and the house in which I was to live was complete with *tatami*, *kakemono* and flower arrangement. But the most impressive was the work in progress – it was like being plunged into a battlefield. Hamada, his two sons and about six workers were glazing and stacking for a firing in the large eight-chamber climbing kiln. There were so many 'firsts' to be taken in at one time; Hamada's decorating techniques, glazing methods, the kiln and stacking and firing, and the men and women in the work crew.

Hamada's workshop is about 30 × 100 ft long with a larger ground area in front of it where pots are dried. Down a steep slope is his largest kiln and another building used for storage of pots and materials – the working area under the kiln shed is about 50 × 50 ft. The entire floor space of all buildings and the adjoining area outside and along the sloping path was thickly covered with boards full of pots! Nowhere was there a clear pathway for walking; men with boards full of pots over their shoulder were nimbly stepping over and around other boards with a weaving over and around each other in a long-rehearsed performance. All glazing was done on the ground, either bending over large wash tubs of glaze, pouring with a ladle, dipping or squatting to decorate and to wash the bottoms of pots. Everyone seemed to know what to do and glided from job to job without being told, anticipating each need and step beforehand. I could only stand in amazement watching this activity.

I later found that about 5000 pots were being fired; most of the glazing, decorating and stacking was done in three working days; this number of pots represented less than two months' work (including bisque firing) by two throwers who have worked for Hamada for ten to fifteen years, his two sons and himself. Extra help is hired for glazing and stacking. The great majority of these pots were thrown, there is no slip casting and the moulds that are used for hexagon and square shapes are exterior, open moulds into which slabs or balls of clay are pressed, modelled and smoothed, each piece therefore being individually worked. One could only ask *how*? Where is the formula by which this tremendous quantity of top quality work can be achieved? For it was top quality. A great majority of these pots were Hamada's, made for coming exhibitions in Kyoto and Tokyo. Others made by his crew were standard stock items for Takumi and other folkcraft shops throughout Japan. Some were orders and others were stock and exhibition pieces to be kept at Mashiko to supply the constant demand of the droves of visitors and sightseers who come there. It is difficult to buy Hamada's work except his top-price exhibition pieces at the many shows given his work throughout Japan, as the demand far exceeds his production.

The kiln firing took two days and the sight of the men stoking small split sticks of pine into each chamber successively, with the resulting belching flames and smoke from the port holes, was highly dramatic. No cones were used, temperature and the dispersion of heat were judged by eye. The kiln was allowed to cool a day before opening, two full days were needed to unload, sort and instruct the packer as to shipments, two more days to finish grinding the bottoms of the pots with handstones, stack saggers and clean the kiln floor and work area. Then work started toward making pots for the next firing.

The workshop is a long stone and plaster building with a thick high-pitched thatch roof which overhangs the building about 6 ft, providing ample space for vats of glaze and materials and drying racks under the eaves. Along the entire length of the front of the building are sliding, paper-covered windows which give the most pleasing light I have ever worked in. There are racks along the back wall as well as overhead, everywhere. In the centre of the earth floor is a 2 ft square bricked depression, a few inches deep. This is the fireplace and serves as a source of heat to dry pots, sandals and oneself, and as everywhere, there is a black iron kettle hanging over it. Running the length of the building under the windows is a bench-like structure about 2 ft high and 6 ft wide. This built-in platform is the only working area other than the floor. No other tables, stools or benches. Interspersed along this structure are 30-inch square holes which accommodate eight potters' wheels; some are Korean-style kick wheels and some are hand wheels turned with a stick.

Hamada's wheel (Photo: Tsune Sugimura)   The potter's tools (Photo: Tsune Sugimura)

In about a week after my arrival, the men were mixing large mounds of clay with their bare feet on the earth floor of the shop, and subsequently throwing commenced. As I watched these small, easy-going men with their relaxed, free movements proceeding in their daily routine of work, I became increasingly aware of our duplication of labour and that our concentration on the technical and mechanical aspect and so-called efficiency has been relatively fruitless by comparison. There is no machinery, no labour-saving thought or devices; the tools are simple and yet they accomplish a greater amount of work with an ease that is unparalleled.

The clay that was kneaded by foot is left on the floor in piles about 3 × 3 × 3 ft at the conclusion of the process. Slices of from 30 to 50 lbs are cut off and wedged on the edge of the platform next to the wheel. Their manner of rolling and kneading, though arduous, is not as strenuous as our method, as they never lift up the bulk of clay as we do when using a wire on our wedging boards. When the final hand-kneading is completed, the resulting rolls of clay are automatically in a handy working position for the wheel. If the clay is too soft, large pats of it are thrown against the stone wall outside underneath the windows and a board is placed on the ground to catch it when it dries and falls off. In every stage of work there is a natural flow of convenience and availability without intellectual planning and organisation. They intuitively use the elements and the materials supplied by nature around them; a wad of dried grass rolled and tied makes the best brush I have seen for washing the bottoms of pots, straw is solely used for packing, and the packer makes much of his rope as he proceeds; pots are dried in the sun and wind, glazing is done outside so there is no thought of drying before firing in the slowly heated kiln, miscellaneous pots and utensils are set under the eave to be washed when it rains, etc.

The Korean kick wheel is a diminutive version of the Normandy wheel. Its construction is simple, consisting of two circular wooden discs about 15 inches in diameter and 4 inches thick, joined together by four posts making a unit about 20 inches tall overall. The lower disc has a 2-inch hole in the centre and the upper one an indentation on the underside. A pointed wooden post is sunk into the ground and the wheel unit is set over it, spinning freely on the point. Some of the wheels have had bearings added to both the lower disc and at the nesting of the point in the upper disc. The wheels are located centrally in the cut-outs in the platform with the wheel head on a level with the platform. The potter sits on the edge of the structure with his feet in the hole and kicks the lower disc, barefooted of course. Some of the potters kick the wheel clockwise as the result of a hang-over from the hand wheel which is always spun clockwise with the right hand for more power. This clockwise kicking is theoretically not considered correct, but it is a matter of preference and habit in the Mashiko area.

Kicking a 15-inch disc instead of a 30-inch one is at first awkward, one's knees are under the chin, and body balance is different, but most of all, there is little power in this light-weight, dwarf wheel which is hovered over. However, in spite of this seeming lack of power, the greater portion of their throwing is done off a 10- to 15-pound mound of clay and the larger pots they make require centring a similar amount of clay. It gradually becomes evident that they do not *push* the clay as we do, but deftly persuade it with a freedom and ease of movement based on sensitivity, skill and a harmonious attunement to the material.

As I watch the throwing by Hamada, or one of his men, or the numerous throwers in the traditional potteries along the roads of Mashiko, the realisation is always the same: the skill and fluidity of movement and the resulting work is the outcome of an approach which is foreign to us. Pots are not *made*, they *flow*. This is best described by such words as ease, naturalness, attunement, non-aggressiveness, etc. There is harmony of living and working, work is not work, it is life; whatever a man is doing, he is doing with his whole being without self-consciousness or even the awareness of physical discomfort or fatigue. When he is throwing, he is completely in what he is doing, when he stops for a smoke, he stops completely. He takes long breaks for tea and shats [sic] and plays with the dog, watches a butterfly or picks a flower to put beside his wheel. But there is never a half-way attitude, always an allness of his whole being. This results in clean, sure movements, always just enough, never indecision and fiddling. Pots grow, are cut and set off, grow–cut–set off with a rhythm of respiration.

Also the importance of acquiring the development and skill to do mass throwing becomes evident. This awareness is based, not only on the usual moral principle of being able to make a sufficient quantity of pots to be able to sell them at modest prices, though this motivation should alone be sufficient, but also on the realisation that in order to make even the *one* good exhibition or 'precious' pot, quality, freedom and ease are related and is therefore the path to vitality of form. Whatever is being made, bowls, pitchers, vases or teacups, when the potter sits and freely throws the same items all day and possibly day after day, it is only to be expected that the first will be stiff and self-conscious, and gradually throwing becomes free and as the pots flow, forms take on a richness and vitality. When the potter is making 50 or 500 pieces of similar proportions, he will naturally lose stiff intellectual thinking, leaving room for feeling and intuition to guide him.

In speaking of skill in throwing, I do not mean mechanical slickness, for Japan has plenty of that also, but rather of an ease and harmony of attitude unencumbered by the awareness that the wheel is a tool capable of producing micrometer perfection. When watching Mr Hamada throw, it is obvious that he is conscious of the nature of the material he is using, clay, and of the form he is envisioning. There are no repressions or regulations governing accuracy or precision relating to the machine. He is striving for the spirit of the form in clay and his working method is always as we observed on his tour in America: the pot comes up and at the first spontaneous burst of life he stops working it. It may not be quite smooth, even or centred but these factors become secondary and he does not sacrifice spontaneous vitality of form to a mechanical slickness and perfection.

Visitors who come to Mashiko are constantly asking me about special clays, glazes, formulas, etc. On the whole, Hamada is using traditional local materials, the same clays and glazes used in the traditional cooking vessels and jars from the area. The glazes are based on wood ash, rice husk ash, pulverised volcanic stone, etc. He makes blendings and small variations but actually the key is the fact that he is an artist and is using natural materials in a creative and intuitive manner. I am fully convinced that were he working anywhere else, using the materials of the area, his pots, though different, as a reflection of different clays, geography and manner of life, would still assume their superior character. This is what being an artist-potter means. It must be remembered that Hamada is a graduate and has done years of research in the best of Western technical methods before crossing the bridge into the realm of natural glazes, basic traditional methods where the spirit of the pot is the primary concern.

An amusing occurrence which exemplifies his lack of precise methodology occurred shortly after my arrival. In the main room of Hamada's house is a square 'fireplace' similar to the one described in the shop, where all the crew, the gardener, the old carpenter and the family gather each morning and afternoon for tea. A kettle is boiled over it, or a pot of soup, as the fire rarely dies. All trash is burned there. [In the] evening as Mrs Hamada was combing the ashes we were amused by the variety of hardware that appears; the metal capping from a Japanese umbrella, small tin ornaments used on the wooden sandal (*geta*) and such. The following week one of the workmen was washing and straining ashes outside the house and when I asked what kind of ash it was, I was told it was from the fireplace!

In about six weeks' time from the previous firing another 5000 pots had been completed, many decorated or slipped with yellow ochre, bisque firing had been completed and we again entered the cycle of glazing and stacking, which again took three days for eight people, myself included this time. Hamada does all of the decoration on his own pots and over half of the decoration on all stock items, plus indicating what is to be done with the others and instructions as to glazes and their treatment. I watched Hamada decorate over 500 pots with wax and glaze in one day as he sat on a low stool with pots around him on the ground. His best pieces were kept until late afternoon and the more he worked the more vigour he had. The work was feeding him rather than draining him.

It is difficult to convey the full meaning of these people's attunement to life and work, but under this atmosphere of natural living and work one does not ask 'How do you glaze this or how do you cut off this pot?', one just does it and it works. This has come to me with a great deal of impact, accompanied by the stark realisation that one may use any natural glaze, any clay, fired at any suitable temperature and realise good pots if the spirit of the work is there. We in America should know this from the examples of Indian, Mexican and early American pottery before us, but knowing is not always fully realising.

I have yet to visit and work in other traditional potteries in Japan, but I understand that in each area the kiln is different, the manner of throwing varies due to the nature of clay in each locality and yet from all these traditional rural potteries, good pots are being made. Obviously it is not the formula nor the temperature nor the method which brings forth the good pot – it is the potter, his life, his personal development and its resulting effect on his use of materials at hand which brings it forth.

Loading the kiln (Photo: Tsune Sugimura)

PLATES 1 & 2
Large dish 1923 (Cat. 7)
Buff stoneware. Lead glaze and
sgraffito decoration
13 × 39 cm

33

PLATE 3
Dish 1922 (Cat. 2)
Stoneware with incised decoration.
Celadon glaze
Diam: 20 cm

PLATE 4
Globular pot 1923–6 (Cat. 1)
Stoneware. *Kaki* glaze
13 x 13 cm

PLATE 5
Bowl 1923 (Cat. 4)
Stoneware. Blue glaze and inlaid floral
design in white clay
12 × 19.5 cm

PLATE 6
Box and lid 1923 (Cat. 5)
Dark brown stoneware. Blue glaze
and inlaid floral design in white clay
9.5 × 6 cm

PLATE 7
Jug 1923 (Cat. 6)
Stoneware. Overlapping *tessha*
and *kaki* glazes
18.5 × 21 cm

PLATE 8
Jug *c.*1928 (Cat. 10)
Stoneware. Dripped *kaki* glaze
17.2 × 21 cm

PLATE 9
Bottle 1923 (Cat. 3)
Stoneware. *Tenmoku, tessha* and *kaki*
glazes with iron brush splashes
28 × 14 cm

PLATE 10
Twelve-sided jar with cover
c.1923 (Cat. 8)
Ash and blue-white glazes
22.3 x 19.7 cm

PLATE 11
Plate *c.*1928 (Cat. 11)
Stoneware. Cream glaze with
kaki spots
5.5 x 21 cm

42

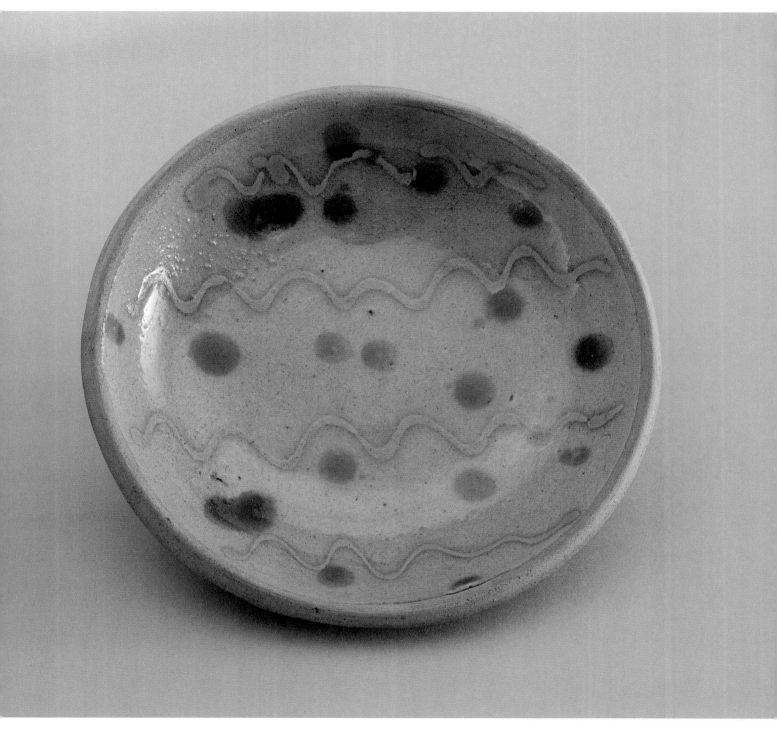

PLATE 12
Plate c.1928 (Cat. 12)
Stoneware. Cream glaze with copper
green lines and *kaki* dots
3 x 20 cm

43

PLATE 13
Teapot *c.*1927 (Cat. 9)
White porcelain
15 x 16.5 x 12 cm

PLATE 14
Bottle *c.*1931 (Cat. 15)
Stoneware. *Hakeme* with
incised decoration
31.8 x 17.8 cm

44

PLATE 15
Flat vase 1930 (Cat. 14)
Stoneware. Iron glaze over wax resist
25.8 × 20 × 12.5 cm

PLATE 16
Bottle c.1929 (Cat. 13)
Stoneware. *Tenmoku* glaze with trailed
slip decoration
35.5 × 16.5 cm

PLATE 17
Large dish c.1940–5 (Cat. 25)
Rice husk ash and black iron glaze
with finger wiped pattern
16 x 49.5 cm

PLATE 18
Teapot c.1932 (Cat. 16)
Stoneware. Black iron glaze
24.8 × 24 × 18 cm

PLATE 19
Round vase 1939 (Cat. 17)
Stoneware. Cream glaze with copper
green and iron splashes
24 × 21 × 18 cm

PLATE 20
Square dish 1940 (Cat. 20)
Stoneware. Cream glaze with red and
green enamel
6.5 x 28 x 28 cm

PLATE 21
Bowl 1942 (Cat. 21)
Stoneware. Cream glaze with iron
brushwork
6 x 20.5 cm

PLATE 22
Teabowl 1940 (Cat. 19)
Stoneware. *Tenmoku* glaze
9.5 x 9 cm

PLATE 23
Teabowl c.1944–5 (Cat. 24)
Stoneware. Cream glaze rim and
interior over transparent glaze
8.3 x 15.1 cm

PLATE 24
Set of dishes c.1953 (Cat. 27)
Stoneware, Rice husk ash glaze
2.8 x 11 cm each

PLATE 25
Food container and lid c.1944
(Cat. 22)
Stoneware. Cream and black iron
glazes with impressed pattern
22.2 × 27.5 × 24.5 cm

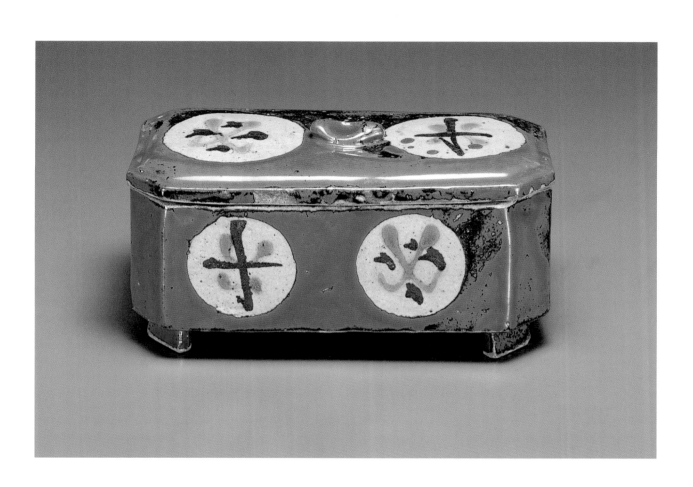

PLATE 26
Box with lid *c.*1940–5 (Cat. 26)
Stoneware. *Tenmoku* glaze.
Copper green and iron rust brushwork
in wax resist circles
10.5 x 21.1 x 11.5 cm

57

PLATE 27
Incense burner c.1944 (Cat. 23)
Stoneware. White glaze with red and
green enamel
7.8 x 9.8 cm

PLATE 28
Incense burner 1970 (Cat. 41)
Stoneware. Saltglaze with
cobalt blue pigment
8.4 x 10.3 cm

PLATE 29
Teabowl 1955 (Cat. 31)
Stoneware. Grey glaze
and iron glaze rim
7.5 x 14.2 cm

PLATE 30
Unomi 1955 (Cat. 29)
Stoneware. Green ash glaze,
incised sugar cane decoration
8.8 x 8.2 cm

PLATE 31
Teapot c.1935–40 (Cat. 18)
Stoneware. Iron glaze with iron glaze
brushwork over white slip
25 × 26 × 18.5 cm

PLATE 32
Bowl c.1950–5 (Cat. 28)
Stoneware. *Tenmoku* glaze with
decoration of leaves in wax resist
20.3 × 23 cm

PLATES 33 & 34
Unomi 1955 (Cat. 30)
Stoneware. *Tenmoku* glaze over ochre
slip, finger wipe decoration
8.8 × 8.8 cm

PLATE 35
Eight-sided vase *c.* 1955 (Cat. 32)
Stoneware. *Kaki* over *tenmoku* over
ash glazes
17.1 x 12.5 x 13 cm

PLATE 36
Jug 1958? (Cat. 34)
Stoneware. Grey-green brushstrokes
over cream *nuka* glaze. Interior with
tenmoku glaze
23.5 × 17.8 cm

PLATE 37
Square vase c. 1965–70 (Cat. 39)
Stoneware. *Nuka over tenmoku glazes*
25 × 12 × 12 cm

PLATE 38
Square vase c.1960 (Cat. 35)
Stoneware. Iron rust glaze over wax
resist sugar cane motif
24.5 x 12.2 x 12.2 cm

PLATE 39
Square dish c.1963 (Cat. 36)
Stoneware. Iron rust glaze and trailed
copper green glaze
6.7 x 30 x 30 cm

PLATE 40
Oblong vase 1965 (Cat. 37)
Stoneware. Iron rust glaze with
copper green drip
22.5 x 15 x 9 cm

PLATE 41
Vase 1969 (Cat. 38)
Stoneware. Salt glaze with sugar cane
motif in iron glaze over white slip
29 x 13 cm

PLATE 42
Tea bowl 1972 (Cat. 42)
Stoneware. White slip with iron glaze
brushwork
9 x 14 cm

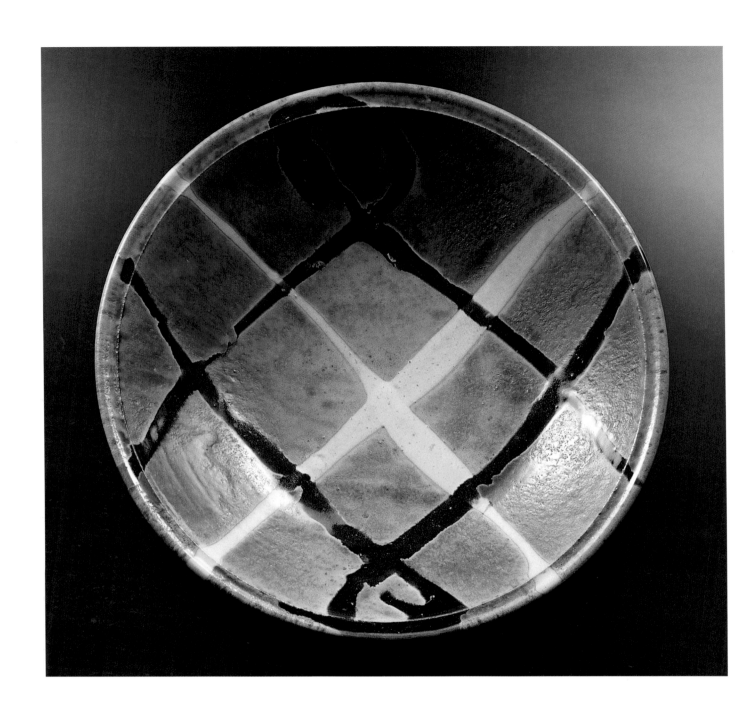

PLATE 43
Large dish 1970 (Cat. 40)
Stoneware. Copper green glaze with
black iron and white glaze trailed
decoration
13.2 x 55.8 cm

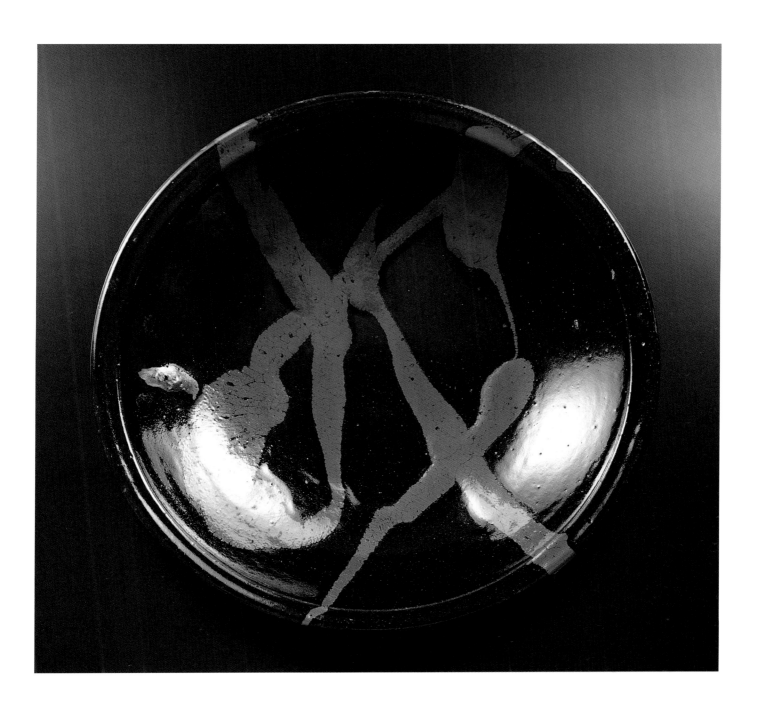

PLATE 44
Large plate 1976 (Cat. 44)
Stoneware. Black iron glaze with iron
rust poured decoration
12.5 x 54.9 cm

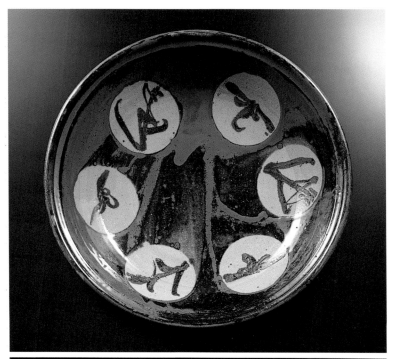

PLATE 45
Large dish 1976 (Cat. 43)
Stoneware. Iron rust glaze with wax
resist circular patterns
13.6 × 55.6 cm

PLATE 46
Large dish 1957 (Cat. 33)
Stoneware. Iron glaze with cross design
in white and copper green glazes
14.5 × 50.5 cm

A NOTE ON GLAZES

Once he was established at Mashiko, Hamada used only five or six glazes, all obtained from local materials. He insisted that these provided sufficient variety and demonstrated it over his 45 years of work there. Towards the end of his life, he did introduce some non-local pigments, such as cobalt blue.

Ame
Greenish brown, obtained by mixing ash with *kaki* glaze

Ash
A variety of wood, straw and reed ashes are used to produce glazes, including the sieved ashes from household hearths

Hakeme
White slip, or liquid clay, usually applied with a brush of bound rice straw

Kaki
Persimmon red, or 'iron rust' glaze, made using a soft sandstone found in the neighbouring village

Nuka
White or cream-coloured glaze made of rice straw ash

Tenmoku
Black glaze made with iron dust from the local blacksmith

Tessha
Dark, plum-coloured glaze used during the 1920s but not in regular use in Mashiko

Hamada decorating
(Photo: Tsune Sugimura)

CATALOGUE OF WORKS

Measurements are given in centimetres (inches in brackets), height × width × depth.

1. Globular pot 1923–6 (Plate 4)
Stoneware. *Kaki* glaze
13 × 13 (5¼ × 5¼)
Southampton City Art Gallery
Hamada and St Ives seals
Purchased from Hamada's 1926 exhibition for £5, but made earlier. Both shape and glazing suggest a particularly early attempt; the piece was nonetheless highly prized by its first owner, Rev. Eric Milner-White, who called it '[t]he work of a master'

2. Dish 1922 (Plate 3)
Stoneware with incised decoration. Celadon glaze
Diam: 20 (8)
Southampton City Art Gallery

3. Bottle 1923 (Plate 9)
Stoneware. *Tenmoku, tessha* and *kaki* glazes with iron brush splashes
28 × 14 (11 × 5½)
The University of Wales, Aberystwyth
Hamada and St Ives seals
Purchased by Sydney Greenslade from Paterson's Gallery in 1923 for £3.5.0

4. Bowl 1923 (Plate 5)
Stoneware. Blue glaze and inlaid floral design in white clay
12 × 19.5 (4¾ × 7¾)
The University of Wales, Aberystwyth
Hamada and St Ives seals
Purchased by Sydney Greenslade from Paterson's Gallery in 1923 for £3

5. Box and lid 1923 (Plate 6)
Dark brown stoneware. Blue glaze and inlaid floral design in white clay
9.5 × 6 (3¾ × 2⅜)
The University of Wales, Aberystwyth
Hamada and St Ives seals
Purchased by Sydney Greenslade from Paterson's Gallery in 1923 for £1.10.0

6. Jug 1923 (Plate 7)
Stoneware. Overlapping *tessha* and *kaki* glazes
18.5 × 21 (7¼ × 8¼)
The University of Wales, Aberystwyth
Hamada and St Ives seals
Purchased by Sydney Greenslade from Paterson's Gallery in 1923

7. Large dish 1923 (Plates 1 and 2)
Buff stoneware. Lead glaze and sgraffito decoration
13 × 39 (5⅛ × 15½)
The University of Wales, Aberystwyth
Hamada and St Ives seals
Purchased by Sydney Greenslade from Paterson's Gallery in 1923 for £4

8. Twelve-sided jar with cover c.1923 (Plate 10)
Stoneware. Ash and blue-white glazes
22.3 × 19.7 (8⅛ × 7¾)
Private collection, UK
Hamada and St Ives seals

9. Teapot c.1927 (Plate 13)
White Porcelain
15 × 16.5 × 12 (6 × 6½ × 4¾)
Private collection, Japan

10. Jug c.1928 (Plate 8)
Stoneware. Dripped *kaki* glaze
17.2 × 21 (6¾ × 8¼)
Southampton City Art Gallery

11. Plate c.1928 (Plate 11)
Stoneware. Cream glaze with *kaki* spots
5.5 × 21 (2¼ × 8¼)
Southampton City Art Gallery

12. Plate c.1928 (Plate 12)
Stoneware. Cream glaze with copper green lines and *kaki* dots
3 × 20 (1¼ × 8)
Southampton City Art Gallery
Purchased by Rev. Eric Milner-White from Paterson's Gallery in 1929; from a set of six in Japanese peasant style, now divided between Southampton and York City Art Gallery

13. Bottle c.1929 (Plate 16)
Stoneware. *Tenmoku* glaze with trailed slip decoration
35.5 × 16.5 (14 × 6½)
The Dartington Hall Trust
Reproduced in M. Rose, *Artist-potters in England*, 1955, plate 29 dated 'About 1930', but more likely included in Hamada's 1929 exhibition

14. Flat vase 1930 (Plate 15)
Stoneware. Iron glaze over wax resist
25.8 × 20 × 12.5 (10⅛ × 7⅞ × 4¾)
Private collection, Japan

15. Bottle c.1931 (Plate 14)
Stoneware. *Hakeme* with incised decoration
31.8 × 17.8 (12½ × 7)
The Dartington Hall Trust
The style of decoration is typical of Okinawa.
Previously thought to be made in St Ives, it has
been suggested by Shinsaku Hamada that this is
an early product of the Mashiko kiln

16. Teapot c.1932 (Plate 18)
Stoneware. Black iron glaze
24.8 × 24 × 18 (9¾ × 9½ × 7)
Private collection, Japan

17. Round vase 1939 (Plate 19)
Stoneware. Cream glaze with copper green and
iron splashes
24 × 21 × 18 (9½ × 8¼ × 7)
Private collection, Japan

18. Teapot c.1935–40 (Plate 31)
Stoneware. Iron glaze with iron glaze brushwork
over white slip
25 × 26 × 18.5 (9¾ × 10¼ × 7¼)
Private collection, Japan

19. Teabowl 1940 (Plate 22)
Stoneware. *Tenmoku* glaze
9.5 × 9 (3¾ × 3½)
The Dartington Hall Trust

20. Square dish 1940 (Plate 20)
Stoneware. Cream glaze with red and green
enamel
6.5 × 28 × 28 (2½ × 11 × 11)
Mashiko Reference Collection

21. Bowl 1942 (Plate 21)
Stoneware. Cream glaze with iron brushwork
6 × 20.5 (2⅜ × 8)
Private collection, Japan

22. Food container and lid c.1944 (Plate 25)
Stoneware. Cream and black iron glazes with
impressed pattern
22.2 × 27.5 × 24.5 (8¾ × 10¾ × 9⅝)
Private collection, Japan

23. Incense burner c.1944 (Plate 27)
Stoneware. White glaze with red and green enamel
7.8 × 9.8 (3 × 3⅞)
Private collection, Japan

24. Teabowl c.1944–5 (Plate 23)
Stoneware. Cream glaze rim and interior over
transparent glaze
8.3 × 15.1 (3¼ × 6)
Private collection, Japan

25. Large dish c.1940–5 (Plate 17)
Rice husk ash and black iron glaze with finger
wiped pattern
16 × 49.5 (6¼ × 19½)
Mashiko Town Office

26. Box with lid c.1940–5 (Plate 26)
Stoneware. *Tenmoku* glaze. Copper green and iron
rust brushwork in wax resist circles
10.5 × 21.1 × 11.5 (4⅛ × 8 × 4½)
Private collection, Japan

27. Set of dishes c.1953 (Plate 24)
Stoneware. Rice husk ash glaze
2.8 × 11 (1⅛ × 4⅜) each
Private collection, Japan

28. Bowl c.1950–5 (Plate 32)
Stoneware. *Tenmoku* glaze with decoration of
leaves in wax resist
20.3 × 23 (8 × 9)
The Dartington Hall Trust

29. Unomi 1955 (Plate 30)
Stoneware. Green ash glaze, incised
sugar cane decoration
8.8 × 8.2 (3½ × 3¼)
Private collection, UK
From the collection of Bernard Leach. Illustrated
in the section 'Exemplary pots' in Leach's *The
Potter's Outlook*

30. Unomi 1955 (Plates 33 and 34)
Stoneware. *Tenmoku* glaze over ochre slip, finger
wipe decoration
8.8 × 8.8 (3½ × 3½)
Private collection, UK
From the collection of Bernard Leach. Illustrated
in the section 'Exemplary pots' in Leach's *The
Potter's Outlook*

31. Teabowl 1955 (Plate 29)
Stoneware. Grey glaze and iron glaze rim
7.5 × 14.2 (3 × 5⅝)
Private collection, UK
From the collection of Bernard Leach and said to
be a particular favourite of his

32. Eight-sided vase *c.*1955 (Plate 35)
Stoneware. *Kaki* over *tenmoku* over ash glazes
17.1 × 12.5 × 13 (6¾ × 5 × 5⅛)
Private collection, UK

33. Large dish 1957 (Plate 46)
Stoneware. Iron glaze with cross design in white
and copper green glazes
14.5 × 50.5 (5¾ × 20)
Mashiko Reference Collection

34. Jug 1958? (Plate 36)
Stoneware. Grey-green brushstrokes over cream
nuka glaze. Interior with *tenmoku* glaze.
23.5 × 17.8 (9¼ × 7)
Private collection, UK
An uncharacteristic shape, perhaps made for
Hamada's 1958 exhibition at the British Crafts
Centre

35. Square vase *c.*1960 (Plate 38)
Stoneware. Iron rust glaze over wax resist sugar
cane motif
24.5 × 12.2 × 12.2 (9¾ × 4⅞ × 4⅞)
Private collection, Japan

36. Square dish *c.*1963 (Plate 39)
Stoneware. Iron rust glaze and trailed copper
green glaze
6.7 × 30 × 30 (2⅝ × 11¾ × 11¾)
Private collection, Japan

37. Oblong vase 1965 (Plate 40)
Stoneware. Iron rust glaze with copper green drip
22.5 × 15 × 9 (8⅞ × 6 × 3¾)
Mashiko Reference Collection

38. Vase 1969 (Plate 41)
Stoneware. Salt glaze with sugar cane motif in
iron glaze over white slip
29 × 13 (11½ × 5⅛)
Mashiko Town Office

39. Square vase *c.*1965–70 (Plate 37)
Stoneware. *Nuka* over *tenmoku* glazes
25 × 12 × 12 (9¾ × 4¾ × 4¾)
Mashiko Elementary School

40. Large dish 1970 (Plate 43)
Stoneware. Copper green glaze
with black iron and white glaze trailed decoration
13.2 × 55.8 (5¼ × 22)
Mashiko Town Office

41. Incense burner 1970 (Plate 28)
Stoneware. Saltglaze with cobalt blue pigment
8.4 × 10.3 (3¼ × 4)
Mashiko Town Office

42. Tea bowl 1972 (Plate 42)
Stoneware. White slip with iron glaze brushwork
9 × 14 (3½ × 5½)
Private collection, Japan

43. Large dish 1976 (Plate 45)
Stoneware. Iron rust glaze
with wax resist circular patterns
13.6 × 55.6 (5⅜ × 21⅞)
Mashiko Town Office

44. Large plate 1976 (Plate 44)
Stoneware. Black iron glaze
with iron rust poured decoration
12.5 × 54.9 (5 × 21½)
Mashiko Town Office

Hamada on the steps of his house in Mashiko
(Photo: Tsune Sugimura)

CHRONOLOGY

1894
Born 9 December, at Misonokuchi, Kanagawa prefecture, his mother's home. His father runs a stationer's shop in Tokyo.

1902
Spends time with Kunizo Hashimoto, a relative studying at Tokyo School of Fine Art, and goes on painting excursions.

1908
Contributes woodcuts to magazines. School prizes for art.

1910
Hamada's vocation towards the crafts confirmed.

1912
Sees etchings and pottery by Bernard Leach in art galleries in the Ginza district of Tokyo.

1913
Enrolls in the Ceramics Department of Tokyo Advanced Technical College. Meets Kanjirō Kawai, two years his senior, at the college. First prize in competition for a woodcut.

1915
During the summer visits Kawai, now working in Kyoto.

1916
Graduates from college and goes to work in Kyoto Municipal Ceramic Laboratory. Visits the potter Kenkichi Tomimoto for the first time in Nara Prefecture.

1917
Visits Okinawa with Kawai to study kiln construction.

1919
First meeting with Bernard Leach at Leach's one-man exhibition in Tokyo. Invited to Abiko, where Hamada meets Yanagi. In Kyoto, makes 10,000 glaze tests. Travels to Korea and China with Kawai.

1920
March: Visits Mashiko for the first time.
June: Arrives in England with Leach. Studies early English slipware in British Museum.
August: Arrival in St Ives.

1921
November: Visit to Ditchling. Meeting with Ethel Mairet, Eric Gill, Edward Johnston.

1922
Matsubayashi comes to St Ives from Japan to rebuild the climbing kiln. Visits to London museums, auctions and antique shops.

1923
April: Exhibition at Paterson's Gallery, Old Bond Street, London.
September: Following Tokyo earthquake, urged by Kawai to return to Japan.
November: Visit to Ditchling with Leach. Exhibition at Paterson's Gallery. Departs from England just before Christmas.

1924
Returns to Japan via Paris and Cairo, arriving in Japan in March. Stays with Kawai in Kyoto and acquires traditional Japanese crafts there; visited by Yanagi.
June: Goes to live in Mashiko, in rented lodgings.
December: Marriage to Miss Kimura and leaves immediately for Okinawa.

1925
January–March: Works in Okinawa.
April: Trip to Isse near Kyoto with Kawai and Yanagi, buying traditional crafts.
December: First exhibition in Japan at Kyukyu-dō, Tokyo.

1926
January: Expedition to climb Mount Koya with Yanagi and Kawai. First son, Ryūji, born.
Works with Kawai in Kyoto.
April: Publication of Yanagi's *Proposal for a Museum of Japanese Folkcrafts*.
In summer, returns to work in Mashiko.
October: Exhibition in Tokyo.
Spends the winter working in Okinawa.

1927
Works in Mashiko and Okinawa. During the winter, further collecting expeditions with Yanagi and Kawai to acquire work to show in the Tokyo Imperial Exposition.

1928
Tokyo Imperial Exposition, with Japanese folkcrafts section organised by Kurahashi and Yanagi, including work by Hamada and Kawai.
April: One-man exhibition at Ishimaru's home in Tokyo.
November: One-man exhibition in Kyukyu-dō, Tokyo.

1929
March: Birth of second son, Shinsaku.
April: Trip to England with Yanagi and Kawai.
May–June: Exhibition at Paterson's Gallery.
Visits Ditchling in August.
Travels around Europe and returns to Japan
in November.

1930
February: 15 works exhibited at Kogukaiten in
Tokyo alongside works of Leach and Ethel Mairet.
September: Acquires his own house in Mashiko.
October: Exhibition in Mitsukoshi, Osaka.

1931
Builds three-chamber kiln in Mashiko (later
enlarged to five chambers).
October: Birth of third son, Atsuya. 144 pieces
exhibited at Paterson's Gallery, 31 October–28
November.

1932
Summer exhibition in Kurashiki, near Osaka.
Travels to Tamba, Matsue and other towns to
study kilns, temples and ancient calligraphy.
Autumn exhibition at Minatoya, a new crafts shop
in Tokyo.

1933
Journey to Sanin and Sanyo, islands off Japan with
Yanagi and Kawai.
October: Folkcrafts exhibition at Yanagi's Tokyo
home, including work by Hamada.
Winter expedition to both northern and southern
Japan with Yanagi and Kawai to study kilns.

1934
March: Exhibition at Matsuzakaya Department
store in Ueno, Tokyo of folkcrafts recently
collected by Hamada, Yanagi and Kawai.
April: Leach visits Mashiko.
August: Travels around Japan with Leach, Yanagi
and Kawai.
November: Exhibition of modern folkcrafts at
Takashimaya department store in Tokyo; the
store's café interior was created by Hamada.

1935
March: Birth of a daughter, Hiroko. Exhibits in
tenth-anniversary exhibition of Tokyo Art
Museum.
May: Exhibition at Little Gallery, London,
22 May–8 June.
November: One-man exhibition at Mitsukoshi,
Osaka.

1936
April: Discovers pottery of Munakata at Eleventh
Kogukaiten exhibition in Tokyo.
May: Travels to China and Korea with Yanagi,
acquiring craft objects.
October: Opening of the Japan Folk Crafts
Museum, Tokyo.

1937
May: In Korea with Yanagi, collecting crafts.
September: Appointed to Board of Folk Crafts
Museum.
November: Exhibition at Mitsukoshi, Osaka.
December: Exhibition at Kyukyu-dō, Tokyo.

1938
January: Birth of fourth son, Ario.
May: Contributes to Japanese folkcraft exhibition.
December: Visit to Okinawa with Yanagi and
Kawai.

1939
February: Death of Ario.

1940
May: Exhibition in Tokyo of work made
in Okinawa.
July: Birth of a second daughter, Hisako.
November: Exhibitions at Mitsukoshi, Osaka and
Tokyo.

1941
Journey to Korea and northern China.
June: First Modern Japanese pottery exhibition.
November: Exhibition at Mitsukoshi, Tokyo with
more than 300 pieces.

1942
Builds an eight-chamber climbing kiln at
Mashiko.
February: Exhibition with Kawai, Serizawa and
Munakata at Japan Folk Crafts Museum, Tokyo.

1943
Exhibitions in Kyoto and Tokyo.

1944
October: Birth of a fifth son, Yoshio.
December: Exhibition at Mitsukoshi, Tokyo.

1945
Continuing contact with Leach leads to suspicion
of spying.

1946
Normal production resumed.

1947
April: Contributes to Twenty-first exhibition of Kogukaiten in Tokyo Art Museum.
December: Exhibition at Mitsukoshi, Tokyo.

1948
Opening of Ōhara Museum in Kurashiki.
December: Exhibition at Mitsukoshi, Tokyo.

1949
Awarded Cultural Medal of Tochigi Prefecture.
December: Exhibition at Mitsukoshi, Tokyo.

1951
Exhibition at Musée Cernuschi, Paris.

1952
Travels as cultural envoy to Italy, Spain and France.
Visits to St Ives.
August: Attends International Crafts Conference at Dartington.
Exhibition at Beaux Arts Gallery, London with Leach.
October: Travels with Leach to USA and gives demonstrations at universities.

1953
February: Returns to Japan with Leach.
October: Exhibition in Niigata with Leach.
November: Exhibition with Leach and Kawai in Osaka.

1954
March: First Japanese Traditional Pottery exhibition at Mitsukoshi, Tokyo.
Exhibitions in Kobe and Tokyo with Leach.

1955
February: Recognised as Living National Treasure, the first award of the title, along with Tomimoto, Arakawa and Ishiguro.
May: Exhibition of work by Living National Treasures at Mitsukoshi, Tokyo.

1956
Thirtieth anniversary of Mashiko pottery exhibition in Sapporo and Utsonomiya.
Continuation of regular annual exhibitions in Tokyo.

1959
Spring visit to Okinawa.

1961
Publication of monograph on Hamada, edited by Yanagi.
August: Leach visits.
October: Joint exhibition with Leach at Daemaru, Tokyo.

1962
Autumn journey to Paris where his work is exhibited in the Louvre.
Becomes Director of Japan Folk Crafts Museum.

1963
Visit to USA to attend joint Japanese-American congress in Washington.
Lectures in New York, Washington and San Francisco.
November: Visits Leach in St Ives. Joint exhibition in Paris, followed by trip to Spain to collect Spanish crafts.

1964
Recently collected crafts exhibited at Mitsukoshi, Tokyo.
May: Exhibitions in Osaka and Kyoto.
August: Work exhibited at National Museum of Modern Art, Tokyo.
October: Exhibition of drawings at Sisaido Gallery.

1965
February: Travels to New Zealand with Atsuya.
Exhibition in Christchurch. Continues on to Fiji, Honolulu, Cairo, Madrid, Barcelona, acquiring traditional crafts.
June: Attends opening of Folk Crafts Museum in Toyama.

1966
March: Exhibitions in Venezuela and Colombia with Leach and Francine del Pierre.
Travels to California, where his daughter is studying, with his wife. All three return to Japan via Europe.
May–October: Leach in Japan.
October: Thirtieth anniversary exhibition of Japan Folk Crafts Museum.

1967
Travels to USA to receive honorary doctorate from Michigan State University.
Exhibition with Leach and del Pierre in Hamburg.

1968
Exhibition in Copenhagen.
Visits St Ives.
July: Awarded *Okinawa Times* prize.

1969
January: Visit to Taiwan.
March: In Okinawa. Visits Hong Kong.
May: Becomes Honorary Citizen of Mashiko.

1970
More than 100 pieces shown at the International
Exposition in Osaka.
Sixth exhibition of work by Living National
Treasures shown in Tokyo, Nagoya, Shizuoka
and Osaka.
September: Work by Hamada shown with
international crafts at Tochigi Hall, Utsonomiya
Prefecture.

1971
April–June: Leach in Japan. Janet Leach's work
exhibited at Daimaru department store, Osaka.

1972
Sekaino Mingei 'Folkcrafts of the World'
published by Hamada.
September: Exhibition at National Museum of
Modern Art, Tokyo.

1973
Awarded honorary doctorate by King's College,
London.
April–May: Leach in Japan. They visit famous
lacquer producing centre of Wajima.
August: Holiday in Scotland.
October: Becomes President of Japan Folk Crafts
Museum on death of Yanagi.

1974
September: In hospital. Visited by Leach who is in
Japan to receive Japan Foundation award. Their
last meeting.
October: *Hamada Shōji's Eyes and Hands*:
exhibition at Tochigi Prefecture Art Museum,
Utsonomiya.
Publication of Hamada's autobiography, *Mujinson*
('Inexhaustible Possessions').
Establishment of the Mashiko Reference
Collection, Hamada's personal museum,
in Mashiko.

1975
April: Leaves hospital. Able to resume potting
in autumn.

1976
May: One-man exhibition in Yokohama.
Publication of a biography in Japanese,
The Father of Mashiko.
Awarded Cultural Prize in his birthplace,
Kawasaki.

1977
One-man exhibition of over 200 pieces at National
Gallery of Modern Art, Tokyo.
Due to worsening health, retires as President of
Japan Folk Crafts Museum.

1978
5 January: Death of Hamada, aged 83.

Based on the chronology compiled by Hiroshi
Aoki and Hiroyuki Mito for the Hamada
Exhibition at Tochigi Prefectural Museum of Art
and Yamanashi Prefectural Museum of Art, 1981.

BIBLIOGRAPHY

Books

Tony Birks and Cornelia Wingfield Digby,
*Bernard Leach, Hamada and their Circle from
the Wingfield Digby Collection*, Oxford, 1990.
Bernard Leach, *Hamada, Potter*, London, 1976.
Bernard Leach, *Beyond East and West: Memoirs,
Portraits and Essays*, London, 1978.
Susan Peterson, *Shōji Hamada, a Potter's Way
and Work*, 1974.
Sarah Riddick, *Pioneer Studio Pottery: The
Milner-White Collection*, York City Art Gallery,
1990.

Exhibition catalogues

*St Ives 1939–64. Twenty-five Years of Painting,
Sculpture and Pottery*, Tate Gallery, London,
1985.
Hamada Shōji, 1894–1978, Ceramic Art Centre,
Mashiko, 1994.
*The English Arts & Crafts Movement and
Hamada Shōji*, Ceramic Art Centre, Mashiko,
1997.